T0150508

IVANA BODROŽIĆ In a Sentimental Mood

COPYRIGHT © 2017, 2021
Ivana Bodrožić

ENGLISH TRANSLATION © 2021
Ellen Elias-Bursać and Damir Šodan

DESING & LAYOUT
Nikša Eršek

PUBLISHED BY
Sandorf Passage
South Portland, Maine, United States
IMPRINT OF
Sandorf
Severinska 30, Zagreb, Croatia
01/7899660
sandorf.hr
knjigolov.hr
contact@sandorf.hr

COVER ART
Shutterstock/Sweet Art

PRINTED BY
Znanje, Zagreb

Sandorf Passage books are available to the
trade through Independent Publishers Group:
ipgbook.com / (800) 888-4741.

Library of Congress Control Number:
2020939185

ISBN 978-9-53351-285-3

First edition
1 2 3 4 5 6 7 8 9 10

IVANA BODROŽIĆ

IN A SENTIMENTAL MOOD

TRANSLATED BY
Ellen Elias-Bursać and Damir Šodan

sandorf • passage

South Portland, Maine

CONTENTS

* Ellen Elias-Bursać
** Damir Šodan

SHOES

Ah what would the simple life be like for us

7

on earth, you and me,
by the Begej Canal,
Begejci, Begejci, Torak
our tongue trips over letters, Romanians, questions,
we walk down a trodden path,
the districts are hidden deep
through the air fly poplars, catkins,
we piss in a dangerous place,
before us they pissed blood,
it was dangerous, nothing written,
no abandoned farms here, says one as he fishes,
his back to us, afterward he yanks the gills off the fish,
sets them on the plastic table on the veranda,
pushes fingers into the toothy hollows, cartilage snaps,
he tells his wife: they've come again, they're asking
again
another, hard of hearing, with clenched fist thrusting
through honeyed air,
saturated with plantlife, fragrant, he has heard of the
abandoned farms,
a few are thataway and thisaway,
you ask for the one where bones were broken,
I can't hear, he says, curves his blackened fingers
around his ears overgrown
with hairs and cupping,
ever since those nights when shrieks sat over the plains
like
misty steam,
steps back to the dirty pillow on the bench in front of
the house,

I don't hear so good, he says, yawns powerless like a
carp from the canal,
they died, all of them died, he repeats
we're looking for the farm, not the people, you shout,
people are born so they'll die,
this we already know

pairs of eyes follow us, hundreds of eyes, from the
gardens, from the windows,
processions, from tractors and trailers, from footstools,
those are my red shoes, I think, but I
don't tell you,
the stupid red shoes I walk with
on grass
shrubs
dust
brambles
while we search for the Begejci camp, who can say
whether such a thing ever was
yet it must have been,
otherwise where would be the beginning of our
love

Easter Island   9
The Navel of the World
Eyes staring at the sky

How did they manage to drag those huge rocks,
the heavy-headed statues,
and who placed them there,
the island offers no clues,
just a few theories—

first they carved them elsewhere,
smoothing out the bottom with unknown tools,
then laced them with ropes from all sides,

proceeding to rock them back and forth—
they looked like walking gods
this must have lasted a while, for one had to calculate
the exact angle, the weight and the force
so they didn't topple

or

maybe they built rails out of bamboo canes,
across a big meadow,
slanted just enough
so the rocks rotated over the wooden blocks
using their own weight

then

the culture of great monuments
was replaced by the cult of "bird man"
leading to most of our sculptures
being damaged or discarded

people devoted their lives to that,
measuring the density, weight, height of Moai
building models
first small ones, then ever bigger, so they could discover
the secret
of Easter Island

we stared at their life's passions,
our eyes shining, distant from each other on that couch,
there was nothing around us anymore,
like when the Little Ice Age
made the forests on the island disappear
or when the Polynesian rats invaded,
eating up all the nuts from what was left of the palms,
but neither of us had the courage to change the channel.

How did you end up here?
they will ask one day when studying us,
so scattered and damaged,
coming up with theories, making models,
as no traces were left behind.

Simply put, it was the era of "bird man" worship.

*

Hot outside?
I said

that might be an ordinary question in May
on the front stairs of a chilly hallway in a building
under that neon lightbulb
that turns everything to the past, into the gray,
experienced long ago

Hot outside
already she'd walked by me as I said the words
stopped with foot midair
glancing at me over her shoulder as if waking from sleep
above, from the mezzanine, I wasn't at that height

Hot outside
and the smile, silly, fake, inappropriate
a moment in her gaze translated into my shame

Yes, a scorcher

answered the third-floor neighbor
who looks through walls, people, her eyes face inward
these last two years
since her husband was killed drunk on the road,
the condolences were of a different hue

Hot outside
was the first thing I'd said,
surprising myself with it
except a barely audible *hi*

and the words in the beginning
anything you need ... what everybody says,
meaningless and superficial

Hot outside
and sticky, and they're forecasting a hellish summer,
disgustingly hot,
and so much has passed, and nothing can be returned,
and I kept my silence till now,
I was scared it might be catching.

Hot outside,
but somehow, she passed by on her way up.

I'd like to plant something that grows,   **13**
let it be full of red juices so you can smear the street
with it.

Let it have its own beginning, its own hard, elongated
seeds
that can be rolled between thumb and forefinger,
sliding down a moist palm,
something that needs
a certain amount
of earth,
moisture
light,
so you know it will continue growing, sprouting a green
shoot, piercing through
the grayness of the seed,
exactly like in those documentaries
they were shooting with the miniature cameras —
first the leaves,
then the ever-thickening stem,
then the miracle of budding,
followed by the mysteries of love and death,
appropriation, pollination, dropping to the ground,
and finally
fruit,
the skin tearing under your teeth, its taste,
precisely defined as cherry
or altogether different like apple,
with no nuances in between
either or
I'd love to plant something that grows,

for I'm tired of all this dissipation, the life-defining nuances,
the incessant yes and no
the could-be and not-necessarily-so
the sure-it-will-happen and maybe-it-never-will.

Just a drop of cherry juice in my throat,
I think, and I'd be saved.

HOLE

My hand went in deeper,
nothing in the way,
no threads, or cloth, or any sort of flat-fell seam.

As in the first collection there is a visible
post-war chronotype diffracting
collective and familiar memory and trauma
entwined with the deeply intimate.

With fingertips I touched skin,
warm, moist
with prickly soft hairs.

The author articulated the text with a lyric expressivity
a stylogenic infantile narrative,
lurking behind the childish voice.

I left it there, in the soft depths,
and then began moving it,
and that spread my lips in a grin,
I squinted, touching the inner side of your thigh.

At first reading, one notices the author's more mature
voice,
perhaps not so much in expression as in
the treatment of the subject matter.

I opened them wide when I heard you not breathing
you were confused, as if you'd like to joke,
but behind your pupils I saw
the color
dark.

From the vantage of point of noticing the polysemantics
and the possible application
of various interpretative practices the creations do not
have this
strength of expression
to evoke in a demanding reader
Barthes's *le plaisir du texte*.

I drew you closer and kissed,
I'd known sooner or later it would have
disclosed its depth to me, so I didn't ask
and wasn't afraid.
The poetess perpetuates certain lyrical devices
similar to those in the first collection, and the reader
may not
wish to read them several times or twice.

For years later we invoked this image
lying in bed, always holding hands,
and again and again you confessed
how you were sheepish about your pocket hole.

The author embarks with agility on self-ironic
metacreativity,
especially in a parodic metatextual game.

I was afraid you'd think all sorts of things about me, you
said,
poor fool and loser, who is incapable of buying himself a
new pair of pants,
so he walks around in torn clothes.

The poem ends with a gag,
wrote the critic, my prof.

Because of it I loved you only more,
and I was happy, truly happy,
when my hand went in deeper.

Jazz is so fragile
I put on a light summer dress
rubbed a drop of perfume between my wrists
(never smear for that's how you destroy the molecules of
fragrance)
and before leaving you kissed me on the back.

We packed up,
—our way—
we selected music for the car,
spread out the map over our knees,
then the earth split open, the road ahead unfurled,
the rivers spilled out of their riverbeds.

It's summer. Everyone's going down to the water,
or else staring up at the light blue sky
welcoming the joy of oblivion, as the trees turn into
carousels,
and we descend, down to the ground,
and a bit further underneath.

What are we searching for, tell me,
as we stand above the tombstone
where Oste and Stojan, father and son,
were buried a long time ago,
whose lives we reconstruct in this game
that only the two of us understand,
as our fingers softly touch our upper-arms.

We did not go out dancing,
over there lies Omarska, how many more sons and fathers,
how many bones below, how many more creak above
still waving, ordering iron to go this way or that.

Jazz is so fragile, my love,
a Time Machine parked amid the main street in Prijedor,
Paris Caffe, Current Jazz, always, mornings and evenings,
except on St. Vitus's Day, the day for celebrating wars
after the monster has already devoured everything,
the way you're showing me with your hands.

Jazz hid itself somewhere,
it rustled its brushes cautiously,
before all those christs and crosses,
before all the loud sons and fathers

below our hotel room window
aggressive men howl,
herding their beasts of steel,
spitting and swearing,
as we shudder underneath a single sheet,
so thin
that every sound hurts, every loud ominous laugh,
pretending we're brave with Coltrane in our ears,
so they can find us ready when they come
to take us to the iron plant,
if need be
to out-scream them
this time around.

IN OUR BED IV

The sounds of your apartment scare me
the endless space of fifty square meters
I didn't conquer
I have only a bed,
and from it I seldom set down my feet.
The fourth bed in my life I call, to myself, my own
and test you and aloud call it yours,
but actually I want you to look at me,
you make it right and say ours.

Something's going on deep inside the wood
in the cupboard door or the window frame,
little sounds warning me it's better not to set my feet
down,
not walk around barefoot while you're at work.
Last night another plane went down,
bodies on all sides, bodies on the screen,
bodies of little children,
like the ones we have, you and I,
and a charred toothpaste box
in the flattened grass, like one you bought not long ago.
On our bed I leaf through a photogallery,
that's exactly what it's called, as if it were something
beautiful
belonging to a Sunday afternoon,
when you come home I won't tell you about it.
Will we have another?
Its chances are a hundred percent zilch,
at the end of the day, again,
we don't know how to talk about anything else.

*

I'm pregnant with a poem
but I haven't told anyone

At night I have cramps in my calves,
in the morning I lie long in bed
because I know, as soon as I get up, I will be pressing my
hands over my mouth.

I lock myself in the bathroom, I observe myself in the
mirror
pull in my stomach, looking for signs in the face
of my eyes.

It's miraculous how they become softer yet more
pronounced,
my hair is shiny, glinting with nuances,
as I let it fall down my back, allowing it to finally grow
long.

I zip up my pants, leaving the top button unbuttoned,
for she is already taking shape, growing a backbone,
her heart has already been beating for a long time.

I don't know if she will have my dreamy eyes
or your almighty hands,
a melon, it will be a boy,
a watermelon, it will be a girl.

I will love her, for she's hurting me so beautifully inside
although everyone will be disgusted by her
once it becomes clear
how round I have become.

Nevertheless, it's the way of the World,
and no one can change it,
for no sooner than we met, I simply knew
this would happen for us.

They're all trying to talk sense into everyone
don't climb onto my bed
don't open my drawer

Answer me when I ask

Don't drink from my glass and don't lean on me
your breath smells nasty

So don't you climb onto mine either

Mommy told me I could, but not you
you're little

Don't rub me like that, it hurts
Don't hold the shower head up high, everything's all wet
Leave the car in gear, turn the wheel carefully
Sweep up the crumbs, ants will come
Empty the pockets when you put things in the laundry
Don't fall asleep fast
you'll ruin everything

Don't cry, not worth it
Don't overdo the oil,
Get undressed, just one more time
Then explain, explain, explain

I said, this is not for you
Don't try and make me laugh
Don't fold the sleeve when you iron
Don't worry about me, go ahead and die of worry
Not that way, this way,
like this and like this

I told you, no, I was telling you,
I'm saying,
I'll tell you when you're,
never again will I repeat

Nobody, but nobody understands anyone else.

SHACK

I heard it from someone else,
about Shack and Shack's wife—
about him selling 20 million copies
of his book wherein God is a witty black woman,
Jesus a gimp with a Semitic face,
and the Holy Spirit an Asian woman

A famous and wealthy writer
who once cleaned toilets
received and dispatched parcels
worked as a night watchman

Anyway,
his wife has strange hair,
although her hair is in fact totally normal,
it's probably that each and every one of us
wants to feel somewhat special
and so does Shack's wife,
never mind how on top of everything
she forgave him for his adultery
which he talks about publicly
as one of the proofs of God's love.

She couldn't find a towel big enough
for that hair of hers in America
(when she wants to wrap it in a turban)
but she did find one in Croatia
so she bought ten of them right away
that now need to be shipped to Oregon

That means that she needs an extra suitcase and she
already has many, way too many things

Shack will travel further, first to London,
then to the Netherlands, then back to London
and then finally back home overseas
for he is a great and famous writer
who goes everywhere, preaching and signing books

Then he leans over to his wife and her extraordinary hair
and says something like:
Darling, don't you worry about a thing,
I'll take care of everything,
I will pick up those right-sized Croatian towels
fly with them to the UK
and deposit them in the hotel safe
so I can collect them on my way back
and bring them
to America
to you

We all laugh, grinning, for Shack is cheap
and his God is a real American product
He loves everybody
punishes no one
and comes in various colors
and his life
including the childhood sexual abuse
is one hell of a tale

When we exhausted our laughter
our faces still in silent grimaces
for a split second we avoided each other's gazes
because his wife
has a husband
who carries towels
for her ordinary hair
across the world

because he believes this is something quite
extraordinary
so passionately
as he believes in God
and no one can convince him otherwise

Faith is Love
Love is God
It's so cheap
yet so unattainable.

*

I'd love to be a father to my daughter
with soft and fragrant little hairs on his hands
so she can bury her nose in them, getting drunk
on something dark, safe and masculine

my feet a size 43 European at least
so she can stand on my toes
feeling taller than everyone else
and not slip down

so she can hide behind my back

and eye me seductively

so I can be her anchor when all else is gone,
her last, very last unconquerable
resort

so I can know how to laugh
mess things up
play chess
and know who Perseus was in love with

how to disappear

for fathers know how to disappear convincingly
while mothers remain to be hated

with twisted lips
and stiff shoulders
bodies generally prone to decay
with very few if any tricks up their sleeve

while hating their own mothers
who never knew
how to father them.

*

I think of Marko while I run
In wintertime the dark starts early
I steer clear of his parents' house
his life tucked into mine.

Someone sent me a message.

Death like life always
finds a way;
technology is just one
of them, like, say,
a text message about suicide.

I sit and wait for an excuse to come
for a funeral,
but all that comes is what was left of him:

he was six, he couldn't pronounce
Nesquik, his sister and I
made him repeat a funny word

he skipped class in eighth grade
and fell in love head over heels
smoked weed like we all did

once spent the night at a police station, his dad left him
there on purpose.

Two old ladies by the graveside chat
about ailing livers,
his life might fit at least three times into theirs

on they natter,
like vultures they've latched on to
the tragedy of a young life.

His sister and I, in a shopping bus on our way to Graz,
she giggles, my nitwit little brother,
he married, at twenty-two
his girl got pregnant
the baby's name is Pablo
we doubled over laughing.

that night Pablo's dad left,
he was only four months old
and all he knew was hunger, being wet and dry,
and when he's dry again he doesn't know a thing.

Days later they found him
on an abandoned soccer pitch.

They only let you see the picture from afar,
she tells me about everything, this way she can bear it,
on the picture you could see him kneeling.

He's quiet. Then for the first time covers his face with
his hands.

All he had to do was straighten his knees.

When he opens his hands like wooden shutters,
transformed
she continues, with a dark gleam in her eye:

God wanted it that way, he knows why.

God comes out like a ghost from a gap of unbearable pain
pain that so fogs the mind,
that Marko's life tucked inside mine,
his bent knees and the noose around his neck,
become a means for his unclear goal.

Paradise is maybe the coolest thing,
that someone could cook up
when there was no longer any other way
to explain absurdity.

I think about Marko while I run
less and less,
it's summer.

TIMELINE

I'll post my picture on Facebook **33**
next summer.

I will take a holiday, not like this year,
I will go to the seaside, rent an apartment,
I will climb a hill with a view on all that
eternal blueness

I will post one of those photos
the sea devouring the sun behind my back
and my shoulders tanned

juice will be dripping from the bursting figs lying on the
tray
but they will not be bruised, rotten or mottled
they will just split in half midline,
and I will capture this with my camera

I will change the profile picture
and get two hundred likes
for that will be one magical photo,
slightly faded
and they will hardly recognize me
in fact, they will be envious
for I will assemble such a powerful gallery
and my friends will be sitting in front of their computers
searching through their folders

but no one will be able to beat
my sunset,
the grains of sand on my feet,
the ancient hunched olive tree,

and I will, if need be, trespass
into someone's yard, snapping photos
of their table, chairs, veranda,
watermelon rinds, parasol,
an open book with folded covers
stained with salt

I will be the happiest one
and it will be obvious
and my children will be happy
posing patiently
wearing angelic smiles
all of us will pose
for as long as it takes
until the veins in our eyes pop
from all that staring into the camera
until our faces grow stiff
until we catch that moment of happiness
so I can post it on Facebook.

Later, we see the crumpled chassis
on the news
cracked windshield glass
drenched in red
like desert roses,
a child's shoe on the sidewalk
a cell phone that
will never vibrate again
black bags
orderlies staring at the ground
crushed grass
the ugly innards of the hood
smashed sooty pipes,
then
lives reaching into infinity
a couple
a mother with two kids
friends going out on the town
a truck driver
young adults
a starring actress
a crooner
a basketball player
a three-month old baby
a legend of journalism
the official cause of the accident
lack of adaptation to road conditions

Often as I drove that way
along a dark stretch of road
I catch sight of the full moon
so starkly dazzling and perfect

with a color for which there really is no word
in our language
magnetically attracting
out of this world
promising,
I stare
my whole body shivers with fear and pleasure
when I realize with an almost negligible sliver of myself
that I've swerved across the solid white line,
I barely swerve back,
go on breathing
and think

well maybe they just saw the moon.

ONE OF MY FAVORITE THINGS

Someone is staring at my back as I stand in a crowd.

I'm bothering someone, I'm all back
blocking someone's view,
though, come to think of it, I don't even know
what my back looks like.

As far as I can see in the mirror
when I really bend;
there are several moles there, those protruding
ones; one of them I tore off
accidentally, with my bra strap;
there were piles of bloody tissues all around me;
Now, there's a little scar there.

I have a twisted spine and certainly
several litres of blood bubbling under
my skin, circling around
and around, permeating everything,
humming,
remembering.

That day when grandma beat me
whipping my naked back
with that crooked stick
as I knelt in the hall banging my head against the wall
because Daddy
betrayed me.
He said:
I'm going to park the car
and left.
Grandma yelled brandishing the stick:

Your head hurts me, your back will hurt you,
so cry, the more you cry, the less you'll piss!

And that time when I slipped down the staircase
landing on my back and hitting the sharp
stair edge, knocking all the air out of my lungs.

And then when I was about to give birth,
I thought my back would break,
but then they stuck that fat needle
right into my back
cutting me in half, so my legs didn't feel like mine
anymore.

And that time when I thought I was very sick,
so, they stuck that needle straight into my back again
extracting a part of me,
that looked blurry and suspicious.

I was afraid I was going to die.

And those little feet stomping
on my back,
made me forget that.

Finally, your palm,
sliding down my neck and lower
as we walk around the city, eyes downcast.

And when the world finally switches off
"My Favorite Things,"
your beautiful big nose
breathing me in
through my back
as my blood quivers

while you nestle your head
underneath my back, soaking up my sweat with your
face
(somewhere down below),
the sweat that breaks out when you take me to that
faraway place,
as I lay on my back, squinting yet seeing everything.

Someone is staring at my back as I stand in the crowd
and wonder
does he see anything?

BREATH OF BRIEF SYLLABLES

Do that in language
Betray
Look long into the sky punctured by the tips of poplars

Give up on words
Retreat into self and remain so in silence
vibrate inside

Despise all versions,
stay indifferent to variants
do not decline, do not quarrel,
pack your mouth with sand

You don't need it
Everything ends, anyway, in silence

The voice is simple, the verb imbalances,
usually it leads to violence,
the subject hopes it matters
and the period at the end seems naive

There is more, there is always more
and there will be more when I'm gone
Say it right, speak distinctly
speak in our language, take a stand

I walk through the cemetery with Mother,
plot no. IV, row III
her words split me in half
they always split me in half
—with me worked two women,
the last name of one was Mijatović, and the other
Mijaaaatović

(and she leans on that "a" to the breaking point)
after a pause she adds,
—that's not the same

Though none of them would know to ascertain
the position of the accent
the length, rising or falling,
or even whether this is a four-accent system
more than 900 of them fit in the pit

A totally minute mark above the letters
stands like that between life and death

Skip it, it's not dignified
quiet
be quiet

MY ONE AND ONLY

I fear I'll stop fearing
for if I stop fearing,
even for just an instant,
I fear something will happen
and not that which I fear the most,
but something else, really fearsome.

So, for as long as I fear,
I'm safe.
I'm horribly afraid
though I know there is no fear,
trembling in the night
is just a small price
I pay
so, I wouldn't fear
what is most fearsome,
the worst thing ever,
the moment that awaits me
if I ever let out a sigh of relief
forget I'm in a state of fear,
and smile naively at someone
in passing,
thus, making happen,
what I fear most.

That's why I'm awake and fearful,
peaceful and secure,
and I caress it, nurture it, soothe it,
so, it can grow big and strong,
to guard me and always be by my side,
my one and only,
my fear.

Your books are gone   **43**
no crutches for remembering
none of your hairs clogging the drain
deep down underground
and stretching out for meters
there are no mattresses with stains of dried fluids
from your body
where you die each night
there is no number you're registered to
confusions about the uniqueness of you
there are no pictures on the walls
to show others
your good taste
no traces of your saliva on cups
nor
a carefully built image of you
made by choice baubles
in the first row on the shelf

In hotel rooms it's home

You are there, unencumbered, real
anxious,
with your bibs and bobs
heaped in a pile
by the head of the bed
so they won't be lost
scattered
forgotten
won't experience your one certain
destiny.

TROUBLE WITH THE STORK

little me is walking down the street
I observe her from the terrace of a café
where I sit sipping beer and writing a poem
first I wave, but she doesn't see me
she is too busy explaining something
with her plump little eight-year-old hands
to her girlfriend who lets her down every other day

her fingers, even when they are grimy with black dirt
underneath her fingernails, smell of butter cookies,
but that won't last long
she doesn't notice me,
she does not even anticipate navel
that crucial tissue for her
only a few meters away

she joined the drama club
one day she'll be a great actress
yesterday she heard of hollywood
she doesn't know if she would go to filip's birthday party
the kid from her class
who told her she's a whore
your mama is a whore
I also told denis in the sixth grade
when he hit me with an ice-pack in the eye
at school we knew that whores had their secret code
wearing red on fridays

those women who cuddle with men for money
really?
she asks me as I turn off the light in the hall

go to sleep, I say
and what are they called, the men who cuddle with
women for money?
go to sleep.

*

I wear my bra when I sleep,
that has stayed with me from the war,
said my mother.

I wear my bra when I sleep,
that's stayed with me from Mother.

Fold your clothes neat on the chair,
said my grandmother,
after a prayer in Hungarian
that tickles me still between
the ears and nose, how those words sound,
that death won't come for you while you sleep.

Fold them nice so you know,
where your pants, socks, sweater are,
in case there's an earthquake,
and we have to run,
everywhere it'll be dark and no power,
you can't go bare-bottomed into the street.

I sleep in socks
but that is different,
blood moves through me slowly,
I sweat only before morning.

But I can't relax any more,
I can't lie there, calm,
the women who bore me slept
too long that way so they could run.

The door is scratching the parquet floor,
they haven't been properly made,
nothing here has been properly made,
the door or the parquet floor.

And when moisture fills the air,
the wood bloats, swells,
and the bottom of the door begins leaving
its semicircle mark on the badly lacquered floor.

The varnish chips off, tiny splinters fly,
the dust settling in its place, along with
dry mud, stuff from the street.

The door needs sanding,
a centimeter, not more,
so I would never have to think about it anymore,
this way, I had to search the whole city
to find someone to help me
with the door, the parquet, the dirt.

Even when there was a flicker of hope,
I had already given up believing the problem
would be solved, thinking if someone does come,
first he will have to remove the door from the hinges,
then take it to his workshop,
find time to engage in that small, insignificant
business of fixing the old door, leaving
all those made-to-measure kitchens aside.

So when that young man showed up
with hands as big as shovels and a bright smile,
he didn't say much.

In a single move he lifted the door off its hinges,
took those round plastic rings from his pocket,
placed them on the hinges and put
the door back in place.

They danced.

This reminded me of your return
for all kinds of things happened while you were gone,
longing devoured me, tears ravaged my face,
eyes wet and swollen, my lips frayed,
evil ruled the world.
This was exactly how it was with that handy man,
like each time you return from a trip.

CYCLE

At the first lecture about sexuality
(the war was raging around us
men were binding women with wire
all across the country)
in the Comrade Tito Conference Hall
sat twelve girls
aged nine to fifteen.

They sent a lady doctor from Zagreb
she came dressed in a white coat
and asked us:
What does "cycle" mean?

I bravely raised my hand.
She signaled me with a look
—that's when you bleed till it stops.

She shook her head gently,
her red cherry shaped earrings
transfixed us
the blood rushed to my face and I wanted to vanish.

The cycle is everything, she said,
from the first day when the egg is released,
and all the way to the last
when it shrivels and falls away,

and the bleeding is
what's in the middle.

The cycle is everything,
the muddy floods in spring
the rainy, rotting summers
and warm winters full of bugs and yellow snow,
bewitchingly beautiful red-hued autumns

endless day is
what's in the middle.

The cycle is everything,
first loneliness
the way I gasp for breath
while you take me by the hand
a grand thought of dying in your arms
my desire for just a little more space
rebellion
and finally
loneliness.

The cycle is everything
a toothless hole in the face
and hard pink gums
full of invisible roots of teeth,
then daily diffusion of enamel
then broken bandoliers
and then again the toothless hole
bleeding is
what's
in the middle.

JESUS LOVES ME

Sunday morning is time set aside
for spiritual experience.
A true believer has no break from God,
the reverend warned us in catechism class.

So I run on Sunday morning,
heading in the opposite direction from the crowd,
bumping into believers
freshly bathed in the Holy Spirit,
returning from mass, neatly combed and purified.

Week after week off they march,
the whole church year around, every Sunday
they scurry in bigger or smaller groups
looking for God.

I search for Him too, by running,
every Sunday morning,
I want to tone my ass
so it can fit perfectly into your palms.

Every time after we've sealed our communion with a kiss,
I climb on top of you,
and you slide your hands over my ass,
lift it gently, remind me to take a peek
at the picture-perfect sight.

Then I hear organ music and smell lilies
and I know that all my sins have been forgiven,
so I believe in Unity
and that's why I cannot take time off
from God on Sunday morning.

*

Forty liters of empties
packed in ones or twos
in a sack I carry over my shoulder

my saliva freezes
between nose and upper lip
salty segment on the face
and bitter in the mouth
is not negligible

in my other hand I tote another dozen
glass bottles clank against each other, chime,
steam rises up off me
the nylon cuts my fingers

I cross the road shining with ice
in the distance I see the yellow headlights of the cars
my jacket is black
and even if it were to happen, if I were to end this way,
the blood wouldn't show
nothing dramatic would be left of me
and I hate you something awful tonight

so I heave one glass bottle after another
into the container
we drank beer and wine
despised each other red, yellow, and colorless
I relish the sound of the smash
this is the festive peak of this day
which I see off in sweats and boots

I heave them in with all my might
and I'm sincerely saddened when it is intact
or just pitifully breaks in half
the sack empties,
but I've only gotten started, just pulled the cork

the plastic ones I set on the ground
let someone else pick them up
milk, oil and the juices of our nervous stomachs
cash them in, buy their booze
let them drink and smash
this is what I have of myself to give.

A DOG'S LIFE

All the sadness of her life
my mother poured, yesterday,
into the tiny corpse
of a twelve-year old bitch
weighing barely two kilos.

She lasted as long
as our love.

In that former life
you came for the first time to visit
by train and I waited for you
at the station with that puppy in my arms.

All kinds of things were happening:
she chewed shoes, a wasp stung her on the muzzle,
she was deadly jealous
when we had a child,
I locked her up in the apartment and took the keys
with me to Dubrovnik,
she would faint every time she met
a bigger dog,
she humped plush toys,
yearning for life and posterity.

Then her teeth began falling out
she ate less
pooped less
the children no longer found her amusing
and I myself changed.

She began stumbling
and growled in other people's presence,
to put her down cost too much,
but the presence of all that suffering
cost us even more.

Then my mother wrapped her up in a towel
and took her away. Her shoulders trembled,
I was ashamed at her crying out loud
and comparing the eyes of the dying dog
with her own mother's eyes.

Once again I thought, without
sharing this with anyone,
that Plato was right, all of this
is just a reflection of a reflection,
this death, this love, this suffering,
we're ever closer to the Idea of it all.

MAN OF CONSTANT SORROW

Men in leather vests,
brown,
interrupt me as I speak,
they don't laugh, except hyena-like and gray.
Usually short arms and legs go along with this,
and fingers on their hands,
worse yet.

And men with long nails,
also on hands;
Even if the fingers are nice,
that won't help.
I shudder even looking at them,
my skin cracks beneath.

And men who are not men,
nor are they women.

Who must have artificial weaponry,
because they don't know how to tell a tale.
Frightened men,
real loudmouths, usually in groups.

Who don't know how to be a brother
they're scared it might hurt,
or a son
likewise.

Men who are never dirty
with uncallused hands, have no scrapes,
the occasional bruise or some such,
though not from smashing but building something.

Who don't put their backs out
except from playing sports, that is, with themselves.

Who don't bathe their children

57
They are only going, going, going somewhere
And they've always gotta go,
Out of time.

Who have to be the first to climax
Because they're unsmart
They don't understand the prize
Nor that they're first, only when they're last
For then they'll always be the first
One and only.

This is why they wear leather vests
And have long fingernails
Engage in many sports
And deal with other men

So that's why you stay home with me.

'ROUND MIDNIGHT

Today, my father's killers have been set free.
I'm drinking with Goga, Petra, Judita, Meri,
Sanja, Izabela, and Ilija.

I laugh as if nothing happened,
As if a twenty-year prison sentence
Has not just been suspended for Saša, Đorđe, Miroslav,
Miroljub, Stanko, and Predrag.

On formal and procedural grounds.

They are also drinking somewhere and laughing,
As if nothing happened,
As if my father's skull with a hole in it,
Is not lying somewhere buried in shallow ground

And I don't know where
But they know

And we're all drinking
And laughing

I drive through a milky fog
I'm going home
Like I'm going to bed

Instead of burying myself in shallow ground, next to my
mother
Then turning on my side
To tell him
Forgive me.

Little size 6 trousers
With bits of lumpy ground meat
From Croatian farms
that ended up in his lap
When I smashed a plate in half at lunch
And all I meant to do was smack it on the table
In his eyes there was nothing
But the deepest surprise

The Hello Kitty sheets are smudged with a brown
Stain of blood that dripped last night from her nose
Because the air was dry,
I was too lazy to open the window, aerate,
Rinse her nostrils with water from the greatest
Depths of the sea
I left it all to time

A shirt, with smells I forgot,
Which I wash only with mine
The jeans that aren't inside out
Pockets crammed with stuff, paper, chewing gum
Infuriate me
I leave them on the bottom for days
Underpants with crusty stains of discharge
Bacterial vaginosis
From a hormonal imbalance
Of an organism at the center of which is sorrow and void
Says the gynecologist.
Unlike me,
She has a holistic approach to my body

A blanket covered in cat hairs
And after washing there are only more
Imprisoned animals without reproductive organs
I battle them for a smidgen of space

I Am the One Who I Am Not
My biography is located
Twenty centimeters left of the washing machine
In the laundry basket

Three times, every week,
I sort into white, color, delicate,
I wash them at hot, medium, cold.

Look at yourself

You are all dirty and scratched,
Draw your legs together when you sit,
Take your hands out of your mouth,
Take them out of your panties,
Suck in your belly
Cover your knees
Lower your backpack onto your ass
Get the hair out of your eyes

Just take a good look at yourself
You are a mess, dark circles around your eyes
You're not sixteen anymore
Don't go out with just anybody
They'll know you've been around
Who will want you like that
When everything down there is as red as a coral reef
Underneath the dark blue sea

Look at yourself
It fooled you, those nights were abuzz like furious bees
You wept them into your pillow
Then come daylight, good morning neighbor,
Wonderful, wonderful, oh yeah, sure
Just look at your children
They're out in the street the whole day long
Sticking their hands in their mouths
Into their panties
Spreading their legs and turning their heads

Just look at yourself
Look at what's left
Of the white tights and the hair clip on your bangs
Look at those tunnels under your eyes
You're done
Look at the abyss in your throat
The laughter is stuck inside and choking you like a bone
In a little while
Fellow cannibals will begin celebrating

Just look at yourself
And admit defeat
So sweet
So sweet like a smashed raspberry on your knee, my dear,
The day is short.

ELLEN ELIAS-BURSAĆ translates fiction and non-fiction   **63**
from Bosnian, Croatian, and Serbian, including Ivana
Bodrožić's novel *The Hotel Tito*. Her translation of David
Albahari's novel *Götz and Meyer* was given the 2006 ALTA
National Translation Award. She is the president of the
American Literary Translators Association.

Born in 1964, DAMIR ŠODAN is a Croatian poet, play-
wright, editor, and translator. His notable poetry trans-
lations into Croatian include the work of Leonard Cohen,
Charles Bukowski, Raymond Carver, Charles Simic,
Richard Brautigan, and Frank O'Hara. He divides his time
between The Hague, the Netherlands and Split, Croatia.

ABOUT SANDORF PASSAGE

Sandorf Passage publishes work borne from displacement and movement that creates a prismatic perspective on what it means to live in a globalized world. It is a home to writing inspired by both conflict zones and the dangers of complacency. All Sandorf Passage titles share in common how the biggest and most important ideas so often are best explored in the most personal and intimate of spaces.